WEAVING GOOD NEWS INTO EVERYDAY LIFE

GOSPEL THREADS

DAVID PLATT

WITH DAVID BURNETTE

ISBN: 979-8-9855655-3-9

Printed in the United States of America

Published by Radical, Inc.

CONTENTS

Introduction   1

Thread 1:
THE CHARACTER OF GOD   7

Thread 2:
THE SINFULNESS OF MAN   17

Thread 3:
THE SUFFICIENCY OF CHRIST   35

Thread 4:
THE NECESSITY OF FAITH   49

Thread 5:
THE URGENCY OF ETERNITY   65

Concluding Questions   79
Notes   84
About David Platt   86
About Radical   87

INTRODUCTION

I'VE GOT TO ADMIT I was a little nervous as we sat in an upstairs room at two o'clock in the morning, surrounded by Muslim men I'd just met, in a country where it's illegal to share the gospel with Muslims.

And yet, there we were, discussing the most contentious, provocative, and even insulting truth of the gospel for many Muslims—the deity of Jesus Christ. Surprisingly, these Muslims were open to listening, and it was because of the way people like Mark, Kim, and Robert were living their lives. These believers had earned the right to be heard by how they worked together in a business that operated in this country. They were honest in their work, and they honored the people they worked with. They also cared for those around them in striking ways. The gospel had been woven consistently into the fabric of their interactions with these Muslims. As a result, people were coming to faith in Christ.

Now you might be wondering, How is that possible in a country where it's illegal to share the gospel?

WEAVING THE THREADS

Mark, Kim, and Robert explained to me that their goal each day is to weave gospel "threads," that is, the core truths of the gospel, into the fabric of every interaction they have with Muslims. In every conversation, in every business dealing, in every meeting, they look for opportunities to speak about who God is and what he has done for them in Christ. Of course, not every conversation involves a full, hour-long gospel presentation. Instead, they constantly aim to weave the various threads of the gospel in their interactions.

The prayer of these missionaries is that, in time, God would open the eyes of Muslim men and women to behold the tapestry of the gospel that has been woven before them. As I watched this "gospel weaving" in action, I was amazed at how natural (or should I say *supernatural*) sharing the gospel could be. But that made me wonder, Why does sharing the gospel seem anything but natural for many followers of Christ?

OVERCOMING OBSTACLES

Why don't authentic followers of Jesus passionately and consistently share him with unbelievers? At least two reasons come to mind, and these reasons get at the heart of why this book was written.

First, some of us don't share our faith because we don't have a firm grip on the core truths of the gospel. Sure, we know Jesus died for our sins, and we see changes in our lives, but things start to get hazy beyond that. We struggle to communicate what the Bible says about God or sin or salvation. That's why this book provides a brief explanation of five major truths, or what we're calling "threads," of the gospel: (1) the character of God, (2) the sinfulness of man, (3) the sufficiency of Christ, (4) the necessity of faith, and (5) the urgency of eternity. These are truths every disciple needs to know. We won't share regularly what we don't understand clearly.

A second reason, and perhaps the primary reason, why we don't share our faith is fear. In many places around the world, there are repercussions for identifying with Jesus. As a result, persecution often silences the spread of the gospel. For those of us who don't face that level of persecution, fear is still present. We fear rejection, and maybe even more so, we fear awkwardness.

The fear of awkwardness is ingrained in many of us. We avoid awkward conversations like the plague. Talk about Jesus at your workplace or bring him up with your neighbor out in the yard, and things can get uncomfortable pretty quickly. But they don't have to. The threads of the gospel are not intended to be an awkward intrusion into our conversations; they're meant to be woven into the fabric of everything we say and do.

USING THIS RESOURCE

In the pages ahead, you'll find an explanation of five different threads of the gospel along with practical suggestions for weaving them into your everyday conversations. They're not intended to be formulas for making all gospel conversations easy. The Bible teaches us to expect indifference, resistance, and opposition to our message (1 Cor. 1:22–23; 2 Tim. 3:12). At the same time, we want to grow in our ability to bear witness to the character of God, the sinfulness of man, and other core truths of the gospel. Hopefully you will be spurred on to think of other ways you can be intentional about weaving these threads.

Finally, as you seek to communicate the gospel with unbelievers, don't forget you're speaking to people who have rebelled against God, are separated from God, and are spiritually dead without God (more on this in Thread 2). That's why sharing the gospel should involve dependence on God in prayer. Only God can save people; only he can soften hard hearts. Our role is simply to weave the threads and trust the Spirit to use them in people's lives.

This resource is adapted from David Platt's sermon series titled "Threads," which can be accessed for free at radical.net.

THE CHARACTER OF GOD

SOMETIMES THE BEST PLACE to begin is at the end. Here's how the last book of the Bible, Revelation, describes the end goal of our salvation:

> Behold, the dwelling place of God is with man. He will dwell with them, and they will be his people, and God himself will be with them as their God. (Rev. 21:3)

There it is, the final reward for every follower of Jesus Christ—dwelling with God forever! In resurrected bodies free from sin, sorrow, or suffering, we will enjoy fellowship with God in a never-ending new creation. That's what he has made possible through the gospel.

But God is not only the end goal of the gospel; he is also its Author. In fact, he is the Author, or Creator, of all things and all people, including you and me (Gen. 1–2). As our sovereign Creator, he owns us (Ps. 100:3). It makes sense, then, that we would want to know this God who created us and who offers us eternal fellowship with him through the gospel. All of us should be asking, What is God like?

Thankfully, we don't have to guess when it comes to God's character. He did not leave us in the dark. As we'll see in this chapter, God has revealed himself to us in his Word, and the portrait is stunning. We'll look at three attributes of God—critical attributes to know if we want to understand the gospel rightly and share it accurately.

GOD IS HOLY

When we describe the character of God to someone, there is no better place to start than with God's holiness. This attribute gets at the heart of what makes God, well, God. In Isaiah 43:15, for example, God identifies himself this way: "I am the LORD, your Holy One, the Creator of Israel, your King."

So what does it mean for God to be holy? It means he is utterly unique, the only One of his kind. He is unlike us, not only because he is the Creator and we are creatures but also because he is morally pure and separate from sin. Yes, we are made in God's image, which means we are in a sense a reflection of him. The Bible refers to believers as "saints" (Col. 1:4), which literally means "holy ones." However, God is also very different from us, for there is nothing wrong in God (1 John 1:5) and he is exalted far above any creature.

When the prophet Isaiah got a glimpse of the enthroned Lord sitting in his heavenly temple, the angels were calling to one another, "Holy, holy, holy is the LORD of hosts; the whole earth is full of his glory!" (Isa. 6:3).

But praising God for his holiness is not only the business of angels. It's a major theme of *our* worship. The psalmist exclaims, "Exalt the LORD our God; worship at his footstool! Holy is he!" (Ps. 99:5). Jesus himself taught us to pray, "Our Father in heaven, your name be honored as holy" (Matt. 6:9, CSB). Our lives, in other words, should be motivated by a desire to see our heavenly Father honored for his holiness. To miss or downplay God's holiness is to have a distorted picture of the God revealed in the Bible.

GOD IS JUST

Another important aspect of God's character is his perfect, inflexible justice. Proverbs 17:15 tells us, "He who justifies the wicked and he who condemns the righteous are both alike an abomination to the LORD."

As a good Judge, God justifies the innocent and condemns the guilty. Injustice is an abomination to him. God only does what is right and just. This picture of God as a perfectly just Judge should stop us in our tracks.

Scripture says God will "render to each one according to his works" (Rom. 2:6), a scary thought given that each of us has fallen short of God's glory (3:23), having been born dead in our sins (Eph. 2:1). So we're left with the Bible's ultimate question: How can a just God look at guilty sinners and call them innocent?

If a judge in our court system knowingly declared guilty criminals to be innocent, we would remove that judge from the bench in a heartbeat. Why? Because he's not just. Likewise, if God simply overlooks sin, his justice and holiness are completely compromised. He is no longer God. We'll see how this tension is solved in a later chapter, but for now we need to see and feel it. A just God cannot simply sweep sin under the rug.

GOD IS GRACIOUS

If God's holiness and justice were his only attributes, we would have no hope. And we certainly wouldn't have a message of hope to share with the world. This is why the third attribute of God, his grace, is such good news. Titus 2:11 says, "For the grace of God has appeared, bringing salvation for all people."

Titus is talking about God's grace as demonstrated in the coming of Christ. But what does it mean for God to be gracious? Grace is one of those words that can seem ambiguous, but it is critical for understanding the gospel.

For God to be gracious means he grants free and unmerited favor to the guilty. He not only spares them the punishment they deserve but also gives them that which they could never earn. Our redemption and forgiveness flow from "the riches of [God's] grace" (Eph. 1:7), and this grace is a "gift" by which we are declared righteous (Rom. 3:24). That word "gift" is important because a gift, by definition, cannot be earned.

Religions all around the world are built on doing certain things, taking certain steps, and observing certain rules and regulations, all to earn the favor of God (or the gods). The good news of the gospel, however, is that God does not require anything from us to earn his favor. As Paul says, "[God] saved us, not because of works done by us in righteousness, but according to his own mercy" (Titus 3:5). Grace, the unmerited favor of God, is our only hope.

WEAVING THREAD 1: THE CHARACTER OF GOD

ACKNOWLEDGE THE GLORY OF GOD IN CREATION EVERY CHANCE YOU HAVE.

→ Talk about God's majesty (in a sunset) . . .
→ Point out God's power (in a storm) . . .
→ Marvel at God's wisdom (in the complexity of our bodies) . . .

ACKNOWLEDGE THE PRESENCE OF GOD IN SPECIFIC FACETS OF YOUR LIFE.

→ God is working in my life (in this way) . . .
→ God is blessing me (in this way) . . .
→ God is leading me (in this direction) . . .
→ God is guiding me (to make this decision) . . .
→ God is teaching me (this truth) . . .
→ God is showing me (this realization) . . .

TALK ABOUT THE HOLINESS OF GOD.

→ Speak about God with reverential awe.
→ Speak about yourself with genuine humility.
→ Draw attention to attributes that distinguish God from people in this world.
→ Draw attention to ways God reigns above the gods of this world.

TALK ABOUT THE JUSTICE OF GOD.

→ Express confidence in God before others, even when things go wrong.
→ Express remorse before God and others when you do something wrong.
→ As you work for justice in the world, speak about the Judge of the world.
→ As you observe evil and suffering in the world, speak with hope about the world to come.

TALK ABOUT THE GRACE OF GOD.

→ Constantly point out evidences of God's grace in and around you.
→ Consistently credit God as the source of everything good in and around you.
→ Continually acknowledge your need for God's grace.
→ Unceasingly express your gratitude for God's grace.

THREAD 1 - REFLECTIONS

THE SINFULNESS OF MAN

WE DON'T LIKE TO admit our own faults. If someone points out we're in the wrong, we often deny it or attempt to shift the blame. It's no wonder Thread 2, the sinfulness of man, is so unpopular.

Like a squeaky-clean mirror, a biblical view of God's character (Thread 1) reveals our unsightly blemishes. It's an unflattering experience, which is one reason many Christians don't want to take an honest look. It's also why they find it difficult to talk about sin with unbelievers. After all, who wants to hear about their own shortcomings? However, people need their sinfulness exposed if they're to see their need for God's grace and forgiveness. A patient will not embrace the cure if he is unaware he has a serious illness.

As we consider the Bible's teaching on man's sinfulness in Thread 2, we'll also find answers to questions like "Who am I?" and "What's wrong with the world?" Such questions are central to every religion and worldview. It's easy to look out at the world and see many things that are wrong: greed, murder, selfishness, exploitation, dishonesty—the list goes on and on. In the face of these realities, the Bible offers a unique diagnosis.

A BIBLICAL PARADOX

The fact that we sin does not mean we are worthless in God's sight. Man is both depraved *and* dignified. I'm convinced this paradox resonates with us at the deepest level. We might state it this way: we are each created by God but corrupted by sin. That statement needs some unpacking if we want to understand it and communicate it to others.

CREATED BY GOD

All people—including unbelievers with whom we plan to share the gospel—have inherent value as individuals created for God's glory and made in his image (Gen. 1:26–27). This distinguishes us from animals, nature, and everything else in creation. God commanded Adam and Eve (and through them the entire human race) to multiply and have dominion over creation (vv. 28–30). Plants and animals don't have this kind of relationship with God.

As humans, we have the capacity for rational thought and moral choice. We have been given a conscience to help us discern good and evil, and we're able to choose between the two. We have a capacity for hard work and artistic creativity; we are innovative and imaginative; we create; we construct; we draw and build, dream and dance, write and make music. We have the capacity for social relationships—we long for love. But, sadly, that's not the whole story. We also have the capacity for sin.

CORRUPTED BY SIN

Despite all our dignified traits, each of us is corrupted by sin. It's a sad paradox: God's image-bearers instinctively engage in sinful thoughts, harbor sinful motives, and commit sinful deeds. John Stott put it this way:

We are able to think, choose, create, love and worship; but we are also able to hate, covet, fight and kill. Human beings are the inventors of hospitals for the care of the sick, of universities for the acquisition of wisdom, and of churches for the worship of God. But they have also invented torture chambers, concentration camps, and nuclear arsenals.

This is the paradox of our humanness. We are both noble and ignoble, both rational and irrational, both moral and immoral, both creative and destructive, both loving and selfish, both Godlike and bestial.[1]

To understand Thread 2, we need to see what it means that each of us has been corrupted by sin. That's a reality we must face squarely if we want to understand and communicate the gospel.

A SOBERING REALITY

Many people feel like their greatest problem in life is something *out there*. Whether it's their job, their marriage, their financial struggles, or something else, they feel unfulfilled due to some external factor. Even many Christians think about sin primarily in terms of what goes on *out there* in the world. However, when it comes to what's wrong with the world, Scripture forces us to look inward.

Everything about us has been corrupted by sin. That's a difficult diagnosis for most people to accept.

After all, who wants to hear about all their faults? We tend to think of ourselves as essentially well-intentioned and good-hearted, even if we mess up now and then. Scripture, on the other hand, paints a much darker picture of our spiritual condition. Consider three aspects of sin's corruption in our lives.

1. WE HAVE REBELLED AGAINST GOD.

Scripture doesn't pull any punches when it describes our sinful rebellion. Amid a long discussion about man's sinfulness, the apostle Paul says in Romans 3:12, "All have turned aside; together they have become worthless; no one does good, not even one." That's a stinging indictment of humanity—some would even say an unfair indictment.

Really, *no one* does good?

The key to understanding Romans 3:12 is to notice that first phrase: "All have turned aside." We have turned aside from God. None of us has glorified God as God. We have all rejected him, and in our rebellion we are reenacting the very first sin on the pages of Scripture. God told Adam and Eve not to eat from the tree, but they did it anyway (Gen. 3). They didn't want God to be Lord over them. And neither do we.

Stop and think for a moment about the God we're saying no to. This is the God who beckons storm clouds, the God who tells the wind when to blow, the God who commands the rain where to fall. He says to the mountains, "You go here," and to the seas, "You stop there," and they do it—immediately![2] Everything in all creation responds in obedience to the Creator, until you get to man. You and I have the audacity to look God in the face and say no. This is the essence of sin: turning from God to self.

Sin reverses the order of God's good design. Instead of putting God first, our neighbor second, and self last, we in our sinfulness put self first, neighbors second (often for our own selfish gain), and God somewhere in the background at a distant third, if he's even in the picture. Of course, we probably wouldn't say "I worship myself," but an honest look at our lives and our vocabulary tells a different story.

There are (literally) hundreds of words that start with self: self-centered, self-esteem, self-confidence, self-advertisement, self-gratification, self-glorification, self-pity, self-applause, self-will, self-motivation, and so on. Apparently we need a rich vocabulary to express the extent of our preoccupation with ourselves. Two ways this self-preoccupation manifests itself are in our self-indulgence and our self-righteousness. See if you can identify one (or both) of these sinful impulses in your life.

Self-Indulgence

Self-indulgence is what we might call the irreligious impulse. Many people rebel against God by living life however they want. They delight in breaking all the rules while they indulge in the pleasures, pursuits, and possessions their hearts crave.

Self-Righteousness

As sinful as self-indulgence sounds, there's an equally sinful and maybe even more dangerous expression of our rebellion against God: self-righteousness. I'm primarily talking about religious people. Regardless of which religion they follow, these people try to do whatever God wants. They strive for good (and for God) by keeping all the rules, assuming that if they live morally, then God will bless and save them. Sadly, many professing Christians fall into this category.

Many who claim to follow Christ believe that if they pray, read the Bible, and regularly attend church on Sunday, then God will show them favor and give them eternal life. But this seemingly "Christian" approach is rebellion against God because it is an attempt to save yourself through good works. Self-righteousness misses the gospel just as much as self-indulgence.

Whether we love to break the rules in self-indulgence or keep the rules in self-righteousness, the core problem is that it's all about us. We want what we want and we (think) we know how to get it. However, what we thought would lead to our good and to our freedom has led each of us into slavery. Jesus said it this way in John 8:34: "Everyone who commits sin is a slave to sin" (CSB). That may sound like an overstatement, but it's how all sin works.

Consider the case of an alcoholic: the man begins drinking and thinks he has found the path to freedom and satisfaction. No one can tell him what to do. But before he knows it, his desire for another drink is out of control. The obsession is literally killing him. The man who thought he was free is actually a slave. And such is the case for everyone who is apart from Christ, for we are "slaves to impurity and lawlessness" (Rom. 6:19). In the end, all our pursuits of joy and freedom apart from Christ are only symptoms of a deeper slavery. We are rebelling against the only One who can satisfy our souls.

2. WE ARE SEPARATED FROM GOD.

The consequence of our sinful rebellion against a holy God is separation from him. This separation, according to Romans 3:23, is a reality for each one of us: "For *all* have sinned and fall short of the glory of God" (emphasis added). We may not want to admit we are separated from God, and we may not always *feel* this separation, but we know instinctively that the Bible's diagnosis of the human condition is true.

Our separation from God is evident in the way we relate to him. We know deep down that something is wrong, and so we recoil from God. We respond as our first parents did in Genesis 3 when sin was introduced into the world. Adam and Eve disobeyed God and they felt the separation acutely:

Then the eyes of both were opened, and they knew that they were naked. And they sewed fig leaves together and made themselves loincloths.

And they heard the sound of the Lord God walking in the garden in the cool of the day, and the man and his wife hid themselves from the presence of the Lord God among the trees of the garden. But the Lord God called to the man and said to him, "Where are you?" And he said, "I heard the sound of you in the garden, and I was afraid, because I was naked, and I hid myself." (Gen. 3:7–10)

Notice how sin leads to shame, guilt, and fear—familiar reactions to each of us.

Shame

After Adam and Eve sinned, they immediately felt shame, and they tried to cover themselves and hide their nakedness by sewing together fig leaves into loincloths. We do essentially the same thing. We try to do good things in our community to make up for our selfishness in marriage. Or we give money to a good cause to deal with the guilt of cheating on our taxes. We might even use religion, hoping our church attendance will mask the sinful things we've done in the past. There are countless ways we attempt to cover over our shame.

Guilt

Adam and Eve didn't only have a sense of shame; their sin actually made them guilty before God. And each of us feels this guilt, for we know we do wrong things. We use various strategies to overcome our guilt.

Many people try to deny there is such a thing as right and wrong. We are free, they say, from fixed moral standards and the guilt that comes from violating those standards. However, no one can successfully erase the sense of right and wrong God has written on the human heart. Our consciences bear witness to the truth. Besides, those who claim that ethics are relative or arbitrary are trapped in a contradiction: they argue it is *right* for you to agree with them and *wrong* for you to disagree!

Another strategy we use to combat guilt is convincing ourselves certain moral standards and expectations are unrealistic. We fail and do wrong because, hey, we're only human. Or there's the claim that certain moral principles are outdated and need to be redefined. Stop living in the ethical Dark Ages, they say. Greed is not a bad thing; it's part of ambition. Exalting yourself is the name of the game, so don't feel bad about it. Lust is natural for men and women, so don't expect sex to be confined to marriage. The list goes on and on.

We deal with our guilt in physical ways as well. Drinking and drugs can serve as an escape for our guilty consciences. Or, as a less extreme option, we turn to busyness, devoting ourselves to games and hobbies and sports so we can make light of our guilt. Perhaps we like to keep the TV or music on all day and night as a constant barrage of sound and sight that guards us from the silence of a guilty soul. Our smartphones have made this a convenient option. Finally, we cover up our guilt with religion and attempt to placate God with our religious performance. We think we can make up for our sins. Yet, deep down inside, despite all our zealous efforts, we know guilt still separates us from God.

Fear

Sin leads not only to guilt and shame but also to fear. Adam and Eve hid from God after they sinned, afraid of appearing before him to take responsibility for their disobedience. This kind of fear is universal. I've seen fear expressed among animistic and tribal peoples who try to keep various spirits and gods appeased through dances, prayer festivals, and sacrifices. Witch doctors and priests hold spiritual sway over entire groups of people who are held captive by fear. While our responses may look different, each of us has fears to deal with— failure, loneliness, emptiness, sickness, pain, disease, or disaster. Ultimately, though, we fear death. The fear of our own mortality, and of what lies beyond the grave, is a reality for every human being.

Our shame, guilt, and fear are the result of being separated from God in our sin. And to make matters worse, this separation is not something we can remedy.

3. WE ARE DEAD WITHOUT GOD.

Dead. That sounds extreme. Could we not just say we have messed up or we need some spiritual healing? After all, we don't always *feel* dead. Many unbelievers are optimistic, kind, and, by outward appearance, full of life. However, the Bible is clear about our spiritual condition apart from Christ: "You were dead in the trespasses and sins in which you once walked" (Eph. 2:1–2). The Bible also refers to death as the wages we have earned by our sin (Rom. 6:23).

Think of sin as our employer: we work hard for him year after year, sometimes with great excitement and sometimes with great disappointment, and yet, at the end of all our hard work, our compensation is death.

This reality of being dead apart from God is expressed in two primary ways: physical death and spiritual death. Every human faces the tragic reality of (eventual) physical death as a result of the first sin in Genesis 3. But physical death is not the ultimate punishment for sin. When the Bible refers to death as our wages, they're ultimately paid out in eternal, spiritual death. That may sound like an unfair punishment, but it makes sense when you consider the One you're sinning against.

God is infinitely just and holy, so committing one sin against him warrants an infinite punishment. And we have committed millions of them! Then, as if things couldn't get any worse, the Bible teaches we are completely unable to save ourselves from this awful condition. A dead man cannot give himself life.

If our problem is simply that we've messed up or done a few bad things, then any religion with a list of good works to do will suffice. But if our problem is that we are dead without God, then only the life-giving gospel of God's grace, a grace that comes *to* us, will suffice. That's why we so desperately need to hear about the sufficiency of Christ in Thread 3.

WEAVING THREAD 2: THE SINFULNESS OF MAN

SPEAK RESPECTFULLY TO AND ABOUT ALL PEOPLE AS INDIVIDUALS CREATED IN THE IMAGE OF GOD.

LOOK INTENTIONALLY FOR OPPORTUNITIES TO ENCOURAGE OTHERS BY THE GRACE OF GOD.

SHARE CONFIDENTLY IN VIEW OF THE REGENERATING POWER OF GOD.

TALK ABOUT OUR REBELLION.

→   Acknowledge the reality of sin in and around you.
→   Acknowledge the root of sin in and around you.
→   Speak honestly about our propensity to sin.
→   Talk about sin in all its forms.
→   Talk about sin in light of its force.

TALK ABOUT OUR SEPARATION.

→   Speak humbly about the seriousness of sin.
→   Let the effects of sin inform the way you talk about salvation.
→   In conversations about guilt, talk about forgiveness in Christ.

→ In conversations about shame, talk about honor in Christ.
→ In conversations about fear, talk about freedom in Christ.

TALK ABOUT OUR DEADNESS.

→ Respond to the death of non-Christians with appropriate honor, biblical honesty, personal humility, heartbreaking anguish, and life-giving resolve.
→ Respond to the death of Christians with profound sorrow, abiding joy, sincere worship, and unshakable hope.
→ Constantly point to our dependence on God (for help, guidance, provision, etc.).
→ Constantly point to our desperation for God (for physical and eternal life).

THREAD 2 - REFLECTIONS

THE SUFFICIENCY OF CHRIST

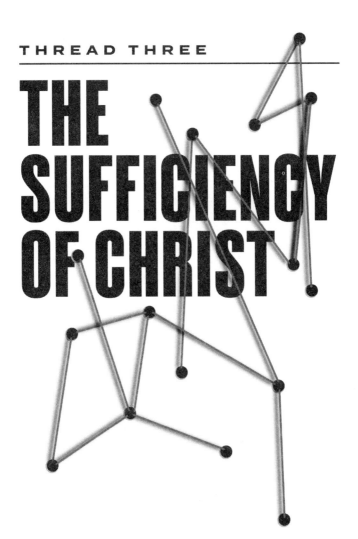

SOME QUESTIONS KEEP US awake at night. Who should I marry? Which job should I take? How am I going to be able to pay my bills? Or, if you're thinking on a larger scale, How can there be peace in a world that seems so troubled and torn? Those are important questions, for sure, but from the standpoint of the Bible, there's a much more important question. It's the most important question, the world's ultimate dilemma: *How can a holy God save rebellious sinners who are due his judgment?*

Unfortunately, that's not the problem most people are concerned about. How many people do you know who are losing sleep over how a holy God can love sinners like us? Instead, most are pointing the finger at God and asking, "How can you let good people go to hell?" They don't give a second thought to the fact that a just God is letting guilty people into heaven.

When we understand the first two threads of the gospel—the character of God and the sinfulness of man—we no longer ask why God finds it *difficult* to forgive our sins. Instead, we start asking how God finds it *possible* to forgive our sins. The fact that God is holy and perfectly just means our sin must be punished (Rom. 6:23). That's what it means for God to be a just Judge. But God is also gracious, showing free and unmerited favor to the guilty (Titus 2:11). So how can God demonstrate his saving love when his just character necessitates condemning us? This tension sets the stage for Thread 3, the sufficiency of Christ.

GOD'S SOLUTION TO THE DILEMMA

We live in a world filled with religious options, and many people believe that, in the end, all of them lead to the same place. No religion is superior or inferior to the others. In fact, the idea that Jesus is the only way to be reconciled to God is perceived as preposterous, antiquated, arrogant, narrow-minded, and even unjust. Surely there's more than one right way.

However, once we understand who God is and who we are, only one solution emerges. Jesus alone is able to remove our sin and restore us to God. So what makes Jesus uniquely qualified for this role? We'll look at the two qualifications that set him apart from every other religious figure in history: (1) who Jesus is and (2) what Jesus has done. Herein lies the key to the divine dilemma.

WHO JESUS IS

Quite frankly, we are dealing with a mystery when it comes to explaining who Jesus is. On the one hand, we see Jesus's humanity. His humble character was apparent to all, for even secular scholars would say Jesus was a good man in religious history. People identify with Jesus because he didn't live a sheltered life. He was familiar with sorrow, struggle, and suffering.

People don't only identify with Jesus—they admire him. Even for us in the twenty-first century, this first-century Jewish figure is attractive:

→ He was loving and kind.
→ He championed the cause of the poor and
  the needy.
→ He made friends with the neglected, the weak, and
  the downtrodden.
→ He hung out with the despised and the rejected.
→ He loved his enemies and taught others to do
  the same.

When Jesus was fiercely and unfairly attacked, he never retaliated. Yet, amid such humility, any honest look at Jesus reveals a corresponding egocentricity.

Jesus was always talking about himself: "I am the bread of life" (John 6:35); "I am the light of the world" (8:12); "I am the good shepherd" (10:11). And Jesus was constantly calling people to follow him (Matt. 4:19; Mark 8:34). "Come to me," he said, "and I will give you rest" (Matt. 11:28). Here we see Jesus drawing attention to his deity, even making extravagant claims about himself. John Stott writes,

> One of the most extraordinary things Jesus did in his teaching (and he did it so unobtrusively that many people read the Gospels without even noticing it) was to set himself apart from everybody else. For example, by claiming to be the good shepherd who went out into the desert to seek his lost sheep, he was implying that the world was lost, that he wasn't, and that he could seek and save it. . . .

These are breathtaking claims. Jesus was by trade a carpenter. Nazareth was an obscure village on the edge of the Roman Empire. Nobody outside Palestine would even have heard of Nazareth. Yet here [Jesus of Nazareth] was, claiming to be the savior and the judge of all humankind.[3]

There is no doubt Jesus believed he was unique and divine. His claims, then, leave us with limited options. If, as C. S. Lewis reminds us, the extraordinary claims of Christ were false and he *knew* they were false, then Jesus was an outright liar. If these claims were false but Jesus thought they were true, then Jesus was a lunatic, a raving narcissist who believed he was the Savior of the world! But if Jesus's claims *are* true, then he is indeed Lord of all. Lewis writes,

> I am trying here to prevent anyone saying the really foolish thing that people often say about Him: I'm ready to accept Jesus as a great moral teacher, but I don't accept his claim to be God. That is the one thing we must not say. A man who was merely a man and said the sort of things Jesus said would not be a great moral teacher. He would either be a lunatic—on the level with the man who says he is a poached egg—or else he would be the Devil of Hell. You must make your choice. Either this man was, and is, the Son of God, or else a madman or something worse. You can shut him up for a fool, you can spit at him and kill him as a demon or you can fall at his feet

and call him Lord and God, but let us not come with any patronizing nonsense about his being a great human teacher. He has not left that open to us. He did not intend to.[4]

There is no one like Jesus, but it's not only who he is that sets him apart. He is also unique because of what he has done.

WHAT JESUS HAS DONE

What has Jesus done that makes him unique? We'll focus on three key aspects of Christ's saving work: his life, his death, and his resurrection.

1. Jesus lived the life we could not live.

Jesus was and is fully human, just like you and me. However, he is set apart from every other man and woman in history because he had no sin. The apostle John put it this way: "You know that [Jesus] appeared in order to take away sins, and in him there is no sin" (1 John 3:5). Unlike us, Jesus never rebelled against God. He was tempted in all the same ways we are, yet he never gave in. He was "without sin" (Heb. 4:15).

It's good news for sinners like us that Jesus experienced temptation, because he can identify with us when we are tempted. He triumphed over sin, not only by going to the cross but also by living a life of perfect obedience to God the Father. Christ is therefore uniquely qualified to be a substitute for sinners, as all other religious leaders stand guilty before God. Guilty people cannot pay the price for other guilty people.

2. Jesus died the death we deserve to die.

As we saw previously, our sin before an infinite God is worthy of infinite condemnation (see Thread 2). Only Christ, God in the flesh, can pay the infinite price due men and women in their sin. Jesus is uniquely qualified to be our substitute because he is fully divine.

The Christian faith puts a special emphasis on the death of Jesus. For other religious leaders in the world, the focus is on their lives, teachings, and examples. Their deaths were the tragic end of the story. Whether it's Muhammad at age 62, Confucius at 72, the Buddha at 80, or Moses at 120, the deaths of these leaders marked the end of their missions. With Jesus, though, it's the opposite.

Jesus was constantly talking about his own death, and the Gospels spend a disproportionate amount of time on the days leading up to his crucifixion. No wonder the central symbol of Christianity for the last two thousand years has been the cross; no wonder the church's gathered worship includes a piece of bread, signifying the breaking of Jesus's body, and a cup, signifying the shedding of his blood. But this still leaves us with a question: How is the death of Jesus good news?

Death is the payment for sin (Rom. 6:23), but Jesus had no sin. Therefore, his death had another purpose:

> He himself bore our sins in his body on the tree, that
> we might die to sin and live to righteousness. By his
> wounds you have been healed. (1 Pet. 2:24)

Jesus died in *our* place for *our* sins. He took the punishment we deserve. If the essence of sin is man substituting himself for God, then it follows that the essence of salvation is God substituting himself for man.[5] That's the answer to the divine dilemma.

God can save rebellious sinners who are due his judgment by taking that judgment upon himself. At the cross, God expresses his judgment upon sin, endures his judgment against sin, and enables salvation for sinners. At the cross, God's holy justice and holy love meet. In holy justice, God fully pours out the judgment we deserve. And in holy love, God, in the person of his Son, pays the price for our sin.

Does God hate sin? Yes—look at the cross. Does God love sinners? Yes—look at the cross.

3. Jesus conquered the enemy we cannot conquer.

I want to be careful not to imply Jesus's death was a temporary defeat, as if the victory didn't come until the resurrection. That's not the way the Bible tells this story. Jesus's death, in and of itself, was victory. God nailed "the record of debt that stood against us" to the cross, and in so doing "he disarmed the rulers and authorities and put them to open shame, by triumphing over them in [Christ]" (Col. 2:14–15).

Jesus obeyed the Father all the way to the cross. The devil never gained a foothold on him. The cross was the victory won, and it set the stage for that victory to be vindicated and declared three days later when Jesus rose from the dead. Hear the triumphant words of Jesus in Revelation 1:18: "I died, and behold I am alive forevermore, and I have the keys of Death and Hades."

This is where Christianity stands or falls—the resurrection of Jesus Christ. If Jesus did not rise, then followers of Christ are "of all people most to be pitied" (1 Cor. 15:19). The resurrection was God's public validation of Christ's life and death. He was announcing to the world that Christ's sinless life and sin-bearing death were acceptable. The resurrection vindicated everything Christ taught, including his predictions he would rise again. Without the resurrection, on the other hand, our entire belief system is meaningless. But if Jesus *did* rise from the dead, then this single event has massive and far-reaching implications for every person on the planet and every person throughout history.

To clarify, when the Bible talks about Jesus's resurrection, it's not talking about resuscitation or reincarnation. Christ was put to death on a cross, prepared for burial, and placed in a stone-sealed tomb. Then, after three days, the stone was rolled away, and the body of Jesus was gone. He was alive, and he appeared (physically) to many people (1 Cor. 15:5–8). That's the kind of resurrection the Bible talks about.

So how should Christ's resurrection affect the way we view him? Consider three ways. First, Christ's resurrection means he is Lord over life and death. No other person can determine how long she lives, nor can she will herself back to life. But that's exactly what Jesus did.

Second, Christ's resurrection means he is Lord over sin and Satan. Satan uses death as a weapon to make us fear, but Jesus has disarmed Satan. Christ destroyed "the one who has the power of death, that is, the devil, and [delivered] all those who through fear of death were subject to lifelong slavery" (Heb. 2:14–15). So whether we face life or death, sin or Satan, we can confidently say,

> "O death, where is your victory? O death, where is your sting?" The sting of death is sin, and the power of sin is the law. But thanks be to God, who gives us the victory through our Lord Jesus Christ. (1 Cor. 15:55–57)

Finally, Christ's resurrection means he is Lord over you and me. This is the fundamental Christian confession in the New Testament: "If you confess with your mouth that Jesus is Lord and believe in your heart that God raised him from the dead, you will be saved" (Rom. 10:9). The resurrection shouts loud and clear that Jesus reigns over us supremely and loves us deeply.

Jesus came to live the life we could not live, die the death we deserve to die, and conquer the enemy we could never conquer—death. And he did all this to save us from our sins. He is a sufficient Savior.

WEAVING THREAD 3: THE SUFFICIENCY OF CHRIST

INTENTIONALLY TALK ABOUT JESUS.

TALK ABOUT JESUS'S LIFE.

→ Look for opportunities to highlight Jesus's example for us.
→ Look for opportunities to acknowledge Jesus's work in us.
→ Look for opportunities to point out Jesus's identification with us.

TALK ABOUT JESUS'S DEATH.

→ Never stop emphasizing the gravity of sin.
→ Never stop talking about your gratitude for Christ.

TALK ABOUT JESUS'S RESURRECTION.

→ Speak about difficulties with hope.
→ Speak about death with joy.

THREAD 3 - REFLECTIONS

THE NECESSITY OF FAITH

IMAGINE FOR A MOMENT that you have a long-lost uncle who is extremely rich. The fortune he leaves behind will be more than enough to cover your needs (and wants!) for the rest of your life. Then imagine that, much to your surprise, this rich uncle mails you a letter informing you he wants to make you the heir of his estate. The house, the cars, the bank account—all of it—will soon be yours! Only one thing stands between you and a massive inheritance.

You have to open the letter.

This unexpected gift will do you no good unless you look inside the envelope. If you toss it in the trash with the junk mail, you will miss your fortune. This generous inheritance is a gift, but it must be received.

We saw in Thread 3, the sufficiency of Christ, that God's gift to undeserving sinners is salvation through the life, death, and resurrection of Christ. However, like any gift, the gift of eternal life must be received. Not everyone is going to heaven simply because Christ died—a sobering reality we'll explore in Thread 5. For now, the question we need to ask is this: How can I receive the salvation God has provided through his Son, Jesus Christ? Answering that question is the point of Thread 4: the necessity of faith.

AVOIDING TWO EXTREMES

According to one poll, about three out of four Americans identify as Christians.[6] That's 75 percent of the country that claims to have faith in Christ, which sounds encouraging. However, the definition of "faith" varies widely, both in our culture and in the church today. Add to that the many different conceptions of God in our culture, and you can see why such statistics can be deceiving. We need the Bible to sort through the confusion.

When it comes to defining faith, we have a dangerous tendency to swing back and forth between two extremes. We either dilute the biblical definition of faith or we complicate it.

DILUTED FAITH

It's possible to so lower the bar for what it means to have "faith" that the word becomes meaningless. Just about every drunk person I've ever met on the street believes in Jesus. Scores of people around the world *say* they believe in Jesus, but their hearts and their lives are far from him. Even demons in hell believe (James 2:19).

We dilute what it means to believe in Jesus when we assume someone is a Christian simply because he or she agrees intellectually with certain truths or says certain words. This error is common nowadays, but it isn't new. Jesus said many people will stand before him on the last day and call him "Lord," and they will even claim to have done great things in his name. Yet, tragically, he will tell them, "I never knew you" (Matt. 7:21–23). This kind of diluted faith is deadly—eternally deadly.

COMPLICATED FAITH

To guard against the error of diluting faith, some well-meaning Christians swing completely to the other end of the spectrum. They complicate faith so much that it becomes difficult to know if someone actually has it. For example, if faith in Christ involves commitment to Christ, how can I know if I'm committed enough? Or if faith involves surrender to Christ, how can I know if I've surrendered enough?

In the process of trying to take faith seriously and push back against the low cost of discipleship in contemporary Christianity, we can unintentionally over-complicate faith. The result is that followers of Christ stay endlessly frustrated or anxious. We desperately need the Bible to give us the right perspective on faith.

GETTING THE RIGHT PERSPECTIVE

We will not understand true, biblical faith until we understand the *goal* of faith and the *role* of faith. These two aspects are captured in this simple (yet profound) summary statement: *We can be restored to God only through faith in Jesus.* We'll begin by unpacking the first part of the statement—we can be restored to God—to identify the right motivation for believing.

THE GOAL OF FAITH

It may surprise you to learn that the goal of believing the gospel is not happiness or joy or peace or satisfaction. It's not even heaven. These things aren't bad, but they aren't the goal of the gospel. The goal is God. Being restored to him is why we come to Christ in the first place. Of course, there are many blessings that flow from being restored to God, not least of which is that our sin problem is dealt with.

You may recall from Thread 2 that sin has plunged man into guilt, shame, and fear. All that changes when we are restored to God. As a just Judge, he cancels our guilt; as a good Father, he removes our shame by adopting us into his family; as a conquering King, he overcomes our fear by conquering death itself. God does all this based on the life, death, and resurrection of Jesus Christ (see Thread 3), which brings us to the role of faith. Our restoration comes only *through faith in Jesus*.

THE ROLE OF FAITH

Many people in our culture claim to have faith, but we need to ask a clarifying question: Faith in *what*? Faith in ourselves? Faith in some vague notion of a God who is watching over us? Faith in our own faith? None of these answers captures the biblical idea of faith, the kind of faith that restores us to God. Let's consider faith in relation to three different aspects of our salvation: the basis of our salvation, the means of our salvation, and the evidence of our salvation.

1. The Basis

We will completely miss the gospel if we do not see that Jesus is the basis of our salvation. We could never stand before God and claim to be righteous on our own, for there is nothing we can do—no matter how committed or radical we might be—to cover up our rebellion against God. We do not rely on ourselves, or even on our faith, to make us right with God. The only way anyone can be declared righteous before God is through someone else's righteousness, namely, Christ's. We are restored to God based solely on the life, death, and resurrection of Jesus.

2. The Means

If Jesus is the basis of our salvation, then what role does faith play? Faith is the *means* by which the salvation of Christ is applied to our lives. If we think of salvation as a gift, then faith is the hand that receives the gift. But why is faith the only means of salvation? Why not love or humility or joy or wisdom? Because faith is the anti-work.

Faith acknowledges there is nothing you can do to make yourself right with God; you must trust in what God has done for you in Christ. Faith is the one attitude of the heart that is the exact opposite of depending on yourself. Faith says to God, "I give up! I can never make myself right before you, so I trust you and depend on you completely to do what I cannot do myself." This kind of faith is altogether incompatible with the idea our good works can somehow give us a right standing before a perfectly holy God. However, as we'll see next, that doesn't mean our good works and obedience are irrelevant to following Christ.

3. The Evidence

If Christ is the basis of our salvation and faith is the only means for receiving salvation, then how do our works fit into the equation? Instead of seeing our works as a way to earn salvation, like other world religions teach, the Bible says good works are the evidence of salvation. Biblical faith necessarily leads to good works. In other words, faith works. That's what the book of James tells us repeatedly: "What good is it, my brothers, if someone says he has faith but does not have works? Can that faith save him?" (James 2:14). The implied answer is *no*, which is why James calls the kind of faith that doesn't produce works "dead" (v. 17).

When your soul is resting upon the grace of Christ, you begin to love as Christ loves, to walk as Christ walks, and to lay down your life for others as Christ laid down his life for you. And these are not works done in some vain attempt to earn the favor of God. You are justified before God based solely on Christ's work; your works are the fruit, or the evidence, of faith.

SEEING THE FULL PICTURE

Having clarified the goal and the role of faith, there's still a dangerous misunderstanding we need to guard against. It is possible to believe that Jesus is the only way to God, and even to want him as your Savior, while refusing to turn from your sin and submit to his lordship. This is what faith looks like for many who claim to be Christians. But it's not biblical faith. As we'll see, there is no faith without repentance. Jesus cannot be your Savior if you refuse him as your Lord.

REPENTANCE AND FAITH

To see the close relationship between repentance and faith, we need look no further than Jesus's first words in Mark's Gospel: "The time is fulfilled, and the kingdom of God is at hand; repent and believe in the gospel" (Mark 1:15).

Repent and believe. These two words show up repeatedly throughout the rest of the New Testament.[7] For instance, when Peter preaches the first Christian sermon, the people are convicted and respond by asking, "Brothers, what shall we do?" The first word out of Peter's mouth is "Repent" (Acts 2:37–38).

However, in other passages we are told to respond to the gospel by *believing*. (It's the same word translated as "faith" in the New Testament.) A Philippian jailer asks the question "What must I do to be saved?" and

Paul responds, "Believe in the Lord Jesus, and you will be saved" (Acts 16:30–31).

"So which is it?" you might be wondering. "Do we repent or do we believe?" And the answer, of course, is both.

Believing in Jesus cannot be separated from repenting of sin. When we place our faith in Christ to restore us to God, we are, simultaneously, turning from sin and self. It's impossible to claim to have faith if we refuse to repent. So what does repentance practically look like?

When we repent, we confess our sinfulness. We acknowledge we have rebelled against God and that we are therefore separated from him. We confess that, apart from his grace, we are spiritually and eternally dead. Instead of attempting to fix ourselves, we admit to God, "I can't fix myself. I have a sin problem only you can solve."

Repentance means not only turning from our sinfulness but also dying to our selfishness. We saw in Thread 2 that the essence of sin is self—putting ourselves on the throne instead of God. To repent, then, is to put God at the center of our lives. Of course, this doesn't mean the struggle with selfishness is over. The temptation to put ourselves back at the center of our lives is always strong, and we must battle it daily. That's why repentance is continually necessary in the life of the believer.

At this point, it may sound as if repentance only has to do with what we turn *from*. But repentance also means turning *to* something—or, more accurately, to Someone. Biblical repentance requires that we trust in

Jesus as Savior and Lord (Rom. 10:9). Trusting in Jesus is not something that may or may not happen after we repent, nor is it something that happens after a certain time has elapsed. Repentance and faith happen at the same time. As we turn *from* sin and self, we turn *to* Jesus. You can't do one without the other; it's a package deal.

SAVIOR AND LORD

Just as biblical faith requires repenting *and* believing, so also it involves trusting in Jesus as Savior *and* Lord. Here's how Paul puts it in Romans 10:9: "If you confess with your mouth that Jesus is Lord and believe in your heart that God raised him from the dead, you will be saved."

Jesus is our Savior, for he is the One whom God raised from the dead, accomplishing for us what we could never do for ourselves. Implied in this reference to Christ's resurrection is his death for our sins (see Thread 3). However, we don't only believe in Jesus as the Savior who died for us. We also submit to Jesus as the Lord who rules over us.

"Jesus is Lord" is a basic Christian confession. That word "Lord" is foundational to Christ's identity as we see it in the New Testament. He is the "Lord of all" (Rom. 10:12), and Paul says everyone who calls on "the name of the Lord" will be saved (v. 13). While Jesus is called "Savior" only twice in the book of Acts, he is referred to as "Lord" 92 times. Without question, the dominant title used for Jesus in the New Testament is "Lord." This idea of Christ ruling as the Lord of our lives is captured beautifully by Paul in Galatians 2:20:

> I have been crucified with Christ. It is no longer I who live, but Christ who lives in me. And the life I now live in the flesh I live by faith in the Son of God, who loved me and gave himself for me.

Paul says he lives by faith in Christ, which means faith is not a one-time feeling or a momentary response that has no effect on the rest of one's life. An initial moment of faith in time leads to inevitable growth in faith over time. To be clear, we are restored to God, or saved, at the moment when we repent and believe. However, genuine saving faith continues to bear fruit in our lives. How could it not if Jesus is our Lord?

Perhaps you're reading this book and you have never turned from your sin and yourself. You've never trusted in Jesus as your Savior and submitted to him as your Lord. The good news is, you can do that now. Simply repent and believe, and you will be restored to God forever (John 3:16). There is an eternal urgency to your response, which is the subject of Thread 5.

WEAVING THREAD 4: THE NECESSITY OF FAITH

TAKE ADVANTAGE OF EVERY OPPORTUNITY YOU HAVE TO TELL YOUR STORY.

→ Keep it simple.
→ Keep it focused . . .
   – On the greatness of God.
   – On the threads of the gospel.
→ Keep it understandable.
→ Be humble and prayerful.
→ Be passionate and be yourself.

TALK ABOUT RESTORATION.

→ In conversations about guilt, talk about forgiveness in Christ.
→ In conversations about shame, talk about honor in Christ.
→ In conversations about fear, talk about freedom in Christ.

TALK ABOUT TURNING.

→ Point to the mercy of Christ when people around you see their sin.
→ Point to the presence of Christ when people around you come to the end of themselves.

TALK ABOUT TRUSTING.

→ Encourage people around you to see the lordship of Christ.

→ Urge people around you to receive the love of Christ.

TALK WITH CHILDREN ABOUT FAITH.

→ Maximize interaction.

→ Utilize illustration.

→ Use repetition.
  - Constantly emphasize the threads of the gospel.
  - Continually encourage a posture of turning and trusting.

TALK WITH CULTURAL CHRISTIANS ABOUT FAITH.

→ Ask thought-provoking questions.

→ Avoid (or at least clearly define) overfamiliar terms.

→ Invite them to study the Bible with you.

→ Expose them to good, gospel-saturated community and resources.

→ Boldly and graciously call them to turn and trust.

→ Intentionally and humbly weave gospel threads.

THREAD 4 - REFLECTIONS

THE URGENCY OF ETERNITY

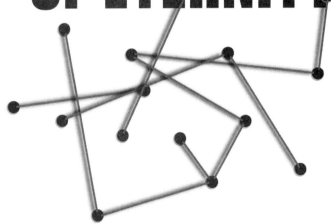

A QUESTION HAS BEEN lying just below the surface in the previous threads, and it's one we can't ignore: What's at stake in our response to Jesus? And why is it so urgent for us to weave the threads of the gospel into our conversations with unbelievers?

As we'll see in Thread 5, everyone's eternal destiny hinges on his or her response to Jesus.

I realize that's a bold statement, but it's the teaching of Scripture. The place where you will spend eternity—billions and billions of years without end—hinges on your response to Jesus. That's why Thread 5, the urgency of eternity, should affect the way we think about weaving the other gospel threads. We need to know what happens to those who turn *from* Jesus as well as what happens to those who trust *in* Jesus. The stakes could not be higher.

A DREADFUL REALITY

When we talk about the destiny of those who are not followers of Christ, we're wading into a subject that's neither popular nor politically correct in our day. The idea that some people will be separated from God eternally in a place called hell is a tough pill to swallow. The world finds the idea of God's judgment either repulsive or irrelevant. Even some professing Christians feel the need to apologize for hell.

Maybe you've heard the argument that hell is only associated with the "God of the Old Testament." Jesus, it's claimed, blazed a more loving trail. However, Jesus did talk about hell—a lot. He told his disciples to "fear him who can destroy both soul and body in hell" (Matt. 10:28). And he warned them of the eternal consequences of living in sin:

> If your hand causes you to sin, cut it off. It is better for you to enter life crippled than with two hands to go to hell, to the unquenchable fire. And if your foot causes you to sin, cut it off. It is better for you to enter life lame than with two feet to be thrown into hell. And if your eye causes you to sin, tear it out. It is better for you to enter the kingdom of God with one eye than with two eyes to be thrown into hell, "where their worm does not die and the fire is not quenched." (Mark 9:43–48)

More examples from Jesus's teaching could be given,[8] but the point is clear: hell is a dreadful reality for those who turn from Jesus. Tim Keller notes, "If Jesus, the Lord of Love and Author of Grace spoke about hell more often, and in a more vivid, blood-curdling manner than anyone else, it must be a crucial truth."[9] The apostle Paul likewise used startling images to talk about God's judgment. He said Christ would come

> in flaming fire, inflicting vengeance on those who do not know God and on those who do not obey the gospel of our Lord Jesus. They will suffer the punishment of eternal destruction, away from the

presence of the Lord and from the glory of his might. (2 Thess. 1:8–9)

This imagery is sobering, and it is all over the Bible. There's a lot of debate about whether the Bible's images of fire, darkness, and destruction are intended to be taken literally or symbolically. But even if these descriptions are symbolic, they are pointing to something literal. The purpose of symbols, after all, is to represent something real, often something difficult to describe. Regardless of how we understand the *imagery* related to hell, the Bible teaches that the *reality* of hell is sure and sobering.

CONTINUAL REBELLION

To some people, hell sounds like an arbitrary or cruel punishment administered by an angry deity. But according to the truths we've looked at in previous threads—particularly God's holiness (Thread 1) and man's sinfulness (Thread 2)—hell is the natural outcome of our rebellion against God and of our separation from him. It's not as if God refuses our cries for mercy. We *choose* to rebel against God, and as part of his judgment, he gives us over to our sinful desires. Hell is a place of continual rebellion against God.

FINAL SEPARATION

If hell is a place of continual rebellion, then it must also be a place of final separation. One of the most sobering aspects of being separated from God at death is its permanence. Hell is eternal. That may sound like an overly harsh punishment, but it fits the crime. One sin against an infinitely holy God is worthy of infinite justice and eternal condemnation. This is the consistent testimony of Scripture.

Jesus refers to a place where the "worm does not die and the fire is not quenched" (Mark 9:48); he calls it an "eternal fire prepared for the devil and his angels" (Matt. 25:41); hell is "eternal punishment" (v. 46). Paul likewise speaks of "eternal destruction" (2 Thess. 1:9). Then, when we get to the last book of the Bible, John says of those who reject God that "the smoke of their torment goes up forever and ever, and they have no rest, day or night" (Rev. 14:11). Reflecting on the eternal duration of God's judgment, the Puritan Thomas Watson said,

> Thus it is in hell, they would die, but they cannot; the wicked shall be always dying, but never dead: "the smoke of the furnace ascends for ever and ever." Oh! who can endure thus to be ever upon the wrack? This word "ever" breaks the heart.[10]

Many people, including some Christians, hear what Scripture teaches about hell and it strikes them as unjust. But before we point the finger at God, we must realize who we are and who he is. God is perfect in knowledge, wisdom, holiness, and righteousness. We, on the other hand, are finite beings who are limited in our understanding. Our thoughts and motivations have been distorted by sin, so we are not in a position to question God. He is the source of all wisdom and knowledge. We must trust that his judgment is always just (Gen. 18:25).

In summary, Scripture teaches that hell is a dreadful, eternal reality for all who have not repented of their sins and put their faith in Jesus Christ. But, by God's grace, hell is not the only option for sinners.

A GLORIOUS REALITY

The good news of the gospel is that although we deserve God's punishment for our sin, he has taken that punishment on himself in the person of his Son. Christ's death on the cross, and his victory over death in the resurrection, gives believers eternal hope. Heaven is a glorious reality for those who trust in Jesus. They can say with Paul, "Our citizenship is in heaven" (Phil. 3:20). And so it only makes sense that we would want to know what heaven is like.

FULL RECONCILIATION

Whereas hell is a place of continual rebellion, heaven is a place of full reconciliation. Hear the words of

Revelation 21:3, the consummation of the biblical story: "The dwelling place of God is with man. He will dwell with them, and they will be his people."

The Bible begins by telling us about Adam and Eve's experience of dwelling with God in the garden of Eden (Gen. 1–2), but this relationship was ruined by sin (Gen. 3). However, when we get to the end of the Bible, we learn that God's dwelling with man will be fully restored (Rev. 21–22). The imagery is glorious: we will be with God, like priests living in the temple, like a bride joined with her Husband, like children united with their Father, like heirs of a King enjoying their inheritance with him, like participants in the banquet of all banquets. These analogies help us see what full reconciliation looks like.

COMPLETE RESTORATION

As if full reconciliation wasn't enough, the Bible tells us heaven is a place of full restoration. We will be completely free from sin, no longer touched by temptation. We will be utterly free to obey.

Heaven is a place where sin will be unthinkable and ultimately undesirable. Yet the reality of *spiritual* restoration should not make us think of heaven as some ethereal land where spirits are playing harps on clouds. Heaven is also a place of *physical* restoration.

Sadly, many Christians find the thought of heaven to be, well, boring. They imagine a static, disembodied existence that lasts for endless ages. Thankfully, God gives us so much more to hope for. The Bible portrays the Christian's final reward as a new earth, a restored earth, where we will eat and drink and work and play and explore and discover new things in glorified, resurrected bodies in an entirely new creation. Our restoration will also be mental and emotional. Mentally, our knowledge of God will be absolutely accurate. Emotionally, our desires will be completely satisfied, and our wants will be totally trustworthy. There will be no conflict between what we want to do and what we *should* do.

ULTIMATE REUNION

In addition, heaven will be a place of ultimate reunion. Heaven is not simply *your* reward as an isolated individual. Paul says "*our* citizenship is in heaven" (Phil. 3:20, emphasis added). This corporate aspect of heaven is captured by the author of Hebrews:

> You have come to Mount Zion and to the city of the living God, the heavenly Jerusalem, and to innumerable angels in festal gathering, and to the assembly of the firstborn who are enrolled in heaven, and to God, the judge of all, and to the spirits of the righteous made perfect. (Heb. 12:22–23)

Heaven is a place where God's people will recognize and love one another as a family before a Father. It will be a reunion of people from every nation and from every generation. We will reunite with those we have known and loved, as well as with brothers and sisters in Christ whom we have yet to meet, and the joy will be unending. This is heaven, the sure hope for all who turn from sin and self and put their trust in Christ.

A CRITICAL RESPONSE

If you've never put your faith in Jesus Christ, then stop and consider what's at stake in your response to the gospel. Eternal life and death hang in the balance. Each of us must answer the question: Will you turn from Jesus or will you trust in Jesus?

TURNING FROM JESUS

There are different ways to turn from Jesus. You can verbally and publicly reject him, or you can agree mentally with the facts of the gospel while refusing to submit to Christ's lordship. You can even be an active member of a church that believes and proclaims the gospel yet still not truly know Jesus Christ. In the end, the result is the same. If you choose to live without Christ now, you will die without Christ forever. But, thankfully, that's not the only option.

TRUSTING IN JESUS

If you turn aside from your sin and yourself and put your trust in what God has done for you in Christ—his life, death, and resurrection—then you can die with Christ now and live with Christ forever.

I urge you to take this second option. Turn from your sin and yourself and trust in Jesus as Savior and Lord. Whether you're 8, 18, or 88 years old, you *will* die, and Satan would like nothing more than for you to be distracted from the urgency of eternity. He loves using TV shows, video games, social media, and anything else that might keep you from thinking about what really matters. Wake up to the reality of eternity. You will either experience eternal joy or you will face eternal wrath.

How will you respond?

WEAVING THREAD 5: THE URGENCY OF ETERNITY

MINIMIZE YOUR CONVERSATIONS ABOUT TEMPORAL THINGS.

MAXIMIZE YOUR CONVERSATIONS ABOUT ETERNAL THINGS.

TALK ABOUT HELL.

→   Speak about God's character with humble confidence.
→   Speak about God's judgment with healthy fear.
→   Speak about God's wrath with honest compassion.

TALK ABOUT HEAVEN.

→   Talk like this world is not your hope.
→   Live like this world is not your home.
→   Talk about your anticipation of being with God.
→   Talk about your realization that dying is gain.

THREAD 5 - REFLECTIONS

....
....
....
....
....
....
....
....
....
....
....
....
....
....
....
....
....
....
....
....
....
....
....
....
....
....
....
....

CONCLUDING QUESTIONS

IT WOULD BE EASY to finish this book and feel satisfied that you've learned a few things or at least been reminded of important truths. Hopefully you have a better grasp of God's character, man's sinfulness, Christ's sufficiency, the necessity of faith, and the urgency of eternity. But to stop there would miss the point.

The goal of this book is not simply to learn *about* the gospel threads, though that is a necessary first step. The goal is to *weave* the gospel threads into our everyday lives and conversations, which is why we need to close by asking three important questions.

1. DO WE REALIZE PEOPLE'S CONDITION APART FROM CHRIST?

Do we really believe that the people we live next to and work with, the people we see in the stores and restaurants around us, are going to hell without Christ? And not just the people we see but also the billions we don't see who have never heard of Christ?

Currently, it's estimated that over three billion people in the world today are considered unreached, which means they have little or no access to the gospel.[11] That's in addition to those who have access to the gospel but have never put their trust in Christ. Unless something changes, these individuals will go to hell forever. We don't have time to waste our lives, our families, or the resources of the church on a nice, comfortable, Christian spin on the American dream. There is an urgency to eternity.

2. DO WE POSSESS THE HEART OF CHRIST?

Knowing people's condition apart from Christ should compel us to weave the threads of the gospel, but that can't be our only motivation. Our passion to reach unbelievers will be shallow and short-lived if we do not possess the heart of Christ. Each of us has been scarred and stained by sin. We've been full of self-indulgence and self-righteousness. But God has changed us. He has reached down his hand of sovereign mercy and saved us from the judgment we deserve. He has transformed our hearts and turned our lives upside down. So the question is, Do we long to see him do the same in others' lives? Surely we who know the love of Christ should be compelled by the heart of Christ to extend that love to others!

3. DO WE WANT OUR LIVES TO COUNT?

Knowing people's condition apart from Christ, and possessing the heart of Christ, will we risk our reputation, face our fears, overcome awkwardness, or do whatever else it takes to lay down our lives for the sake of the gospel? It's the kind of perspective that says with the apostle Paul,

> I do not account my life of any value nor as precious to myself, if only I may finish my course and the ministry that I received from the Lord Jesus, to testify to the gospel of the grace of God. (Acts 20:24)

Paul didn't care about comfort, safety, or security in this world. Instead, he wanted his life to count for the spread of the gospel. Will we look back ten trillion years from now and wish we'd made more money? Wish we'd been more comfortable? Wish we'd lived more for ourselves? We stand on the porch of eternity. John Piper writes,

> When you know the truth about what happens to you after you die, and you believe it, and you are satisfied with all that God will be for you in the ages to come, that truth makes you free indeed. Free from the short, shallow, suicidal pleasures of sin, and free for the sacrifices of mission and ministry that cause people to give glory to our Father in heaven.[12]

Surrender your life to God and ask him to make it count for the spread of his gospel in your city and to the ends of the earth. This is the only reasonable reaction for those who believe in the character of God, the sinfulness of man, the sufficiency of Christ, the necessity of faith, and the urgency of eternity. Let's weave these threads and ask God to use them for others' eternal good and for his eternal glory.

CONCLUDING REFLECTIONS

NOTES

1. John Stott, *Why I Am a Christian* (Downers Grove, IL: Inter-Varsity Press, 2014), 76.
2. For examples of God's sovereign lordship over creation, see Job 38:8–11; Psalm 135:6–7; 147:8; 148:7–10. See also Jesus's lordship over the winds and sea in Matthew 8:26.
3. Stott, *Why I Am a Christian*, 42–43.
4. C. S. Lewis, *Mere Christianity* (London: William Collins, 2016), 52.
5. John Stott, *The Cross of Christ* (Nottingham: InterVarsity Press, 2006), 188.
6. Frank Newport, "Percentage of Christians in U.S. Drifting Down, but Still High," Gallup, December 24, 2015, www.gallup.com/poll/187955/percentage-christians-drifting-down-high.aspx.
7. See the emphasis on repentance in the book of Acts as the gospel spreads across the known world: Acts 3:19; 5:31; 8:22; 17:30; 26:20.
8. For other examples where Jesus refers to hell, see the following passages: Matthew 5:22, 29, 30; 16:18; 18:9; 23:15, 33; Luke 12:5.
9. Tim Keller, "The Importance of Hell," The Redeemer Reports, Redeemer Presbyterian Church, August 2009, www.redeemer.com/redeemer-report/article/the_importance_of_hell.
10. *Farewell Sermons of Some of the Most Eminent of the Nonconformist Preachers* (London: Gale and Fenner, 1816), 220, https://archive.org/details/cu31924029358789.

11. For statistics related to unreached people groups and places, see joshuaproject.net and stratus.earth. To learn more about the term "unreached," see the article titled "Who Are Unreached People Groups?" at radical.net.

12. John Piper, *Future Grace: The Purifying Power of the Promises of God*, rev. ed. (Colorado Springs: Multnomah Books, 2012), 369–70.

ABOUT DAVID PLATT

David Platt serves as a pastor in metro Washington, DC. He is the founder of Radical.

David received his PhD from New Orleans Baptist Theological Seminary and is the author of *Don't Hold Back*, *Radical*, *Follow Me*, *Counter Culture*, *Something Needs to Change*, and *Before You Vote*, as well as multiple volumes of the *Christ-Centered Exposition Commentary* series.

Along with his wife and children, he lives in the Washington, DC, metro area.

ABOUT RADICAL

Radical serves the church by equipping Christians to follow Jesus and to make him known in their neighborhoods and among all nations. In places where the gospel is already accessible, we work to awaken and mobilize the church. In areas where access is limited, we work to advance the gospel and see churches planted.

To learn more and get involved, visit us online at radical.net.

URGENT

Make Christ Known Among The Unreached

 give today   radical.net/urgent-needs

Over 20 Secret Church Events To Explore

Stream video, download study guides and answer keys,
transcripts, discussion guides, and more all for free!

 radical.net/sc

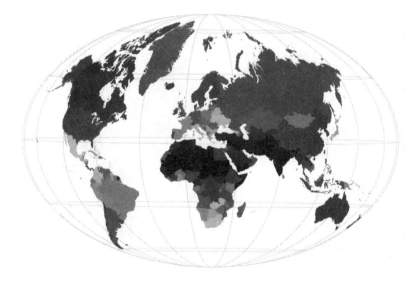

RADICAL
TRAINING

An immersive 8-month program to equip
participants for the spread of the gospel.

Apply Today   radical.net/radical-training

NEIGHBORHOODS &NATIONS

Stories of God's work around the world

radical.net/nn